○

ICONICOSMICA

b
y

t
r
a
n
s
i
e
n
c
e

✦ ✦
✧

ISBN 978-0-578-83918-9

© 2023 iconicosmica
iconicosmica.com

transience

impermanence
does not
make
living
a waste

eternity
is fixed

but transience
breathes .
grows

bleeding
and beautiful

♯
F
F
F
F
F
F

◇

adventure

to exist is neither good nor bad

but a prismatic experience defined by variation

each shade in response to the spectrum

of a diamond shining inspiration

its facets refracting the path of a life

rising before you from the abyss

into the horizon lies the answer

it's better to find out than to wonder

for as it is discovered

life is an adventure

♯
C
4
5
F
B
F

phoenix

i open and close
like the jaws of a cat

wander too close
and i'll bite you in half

i expand and contract
like the lungs sigh for breath

fighting for air until
flowers are left

i rise and then fall
like i'm chasing the sun

where i follow the path
toward the horizon

i destroy everything
by resembling creation

reflecting perfect
as a diamond

i'm there at the beginning
after causing the end

i bathe in the blood
that was spilt from my skin

i shatter idols
to model my body
i grab on my titties
and straddle myself

i eat of the fruit just
to know how it tastes

then i am born new
from the ashes of fate

♯
F
0
4
7
5
3

◇

solace

ı've been trapped here so long ı've forgotten why

at some point ı wandered into this abyss . ı was tossed . or maybe fell . ı have gleams of what may have happened . stirring intangibly from memory . but nothing ı can recover as evidence . for a history unknown to me . visions ı confuse with reality . locked in a realm that exists without rhyme . there is no certainty of anything but my mind

except for this solace . twinkling upon the aurora . a singularity . nir light the only destination . but no matter how ı call to the source for escape . ı can never seem to obtain it . always evading my grasp . among infinite emptiness there's simply nothing to reach toward . yearning has become the sole reminder ı exist . in a body foreign to me . time doesn't really pass at all . in an eternity without resolve

eventually there is a response to my prayer . written in the void at the start of everything .

this relationship formed between me and the star . hovering above us and I never noticed . always so distracted by the thought of tomorrow . that I forget to acknowledge revelations of the past . until now illumination has finally arrived . I can recognize this wish was granted long ago . a celestial being wearing a mask . paper grey with features ink . eyes winking the astralis . feathered ne returns here as a spirit . answering beyond reality

I *am the nightengale* ne croons . craning in a cloak of silence

who are you I echo . as if interpreting myself

everything and nothing

will you guide me through the ether I plead

I *am merely projection* ne wrinkles *you already know the way*

the nightengale raises nir lantern . a prism through which the light gets refracted . in every shade to form a spectrum infinite . colors banding together as a bridge to the sun . lighting a stair from heaven . hues unseen banishing the darkness grateful I am drawn into this morning . as dawn ascends over the planet . dragging me toward it . a carriage awaits near the entrance . where castle gates sparkle enchantment . the nightengale perched at the helm of it . staring impassive until I am mounted next to nem . uncertain with the reigns . there seems to be more freedom than I can handle . shadows creeping in my rearview

it is destiny

I begin with a jolt . power coursing through my veins . as if the chariot were a battery . charging across infinite regions . we don't glide so much as fall . the rainbow pulled by some gravity . an attractor from another universe . that we're fated to meet . for all I must do is rise into place

with a flutter of wings we traverse the scale of this diamond . mountains and valleys converging around us as a series of mirrors and windows . displaying the object and subjective . like perceiving through a kaleidoscope . the iris bows before me in an arc to the horizon . where imagination discovers unlimited potential . casting depth from the shallows . I seem to experience everything as an extension of myself . with arms spread open to receive the world . the domain of it expanding endlessly

do you know how we came to be here the nightengale ponders from beside me

perhaps . but ɪ can't tell the truth from nothing

the reason is absence

ɪ choose to ignore it . reckoning nir words along the path . until ɪ am lost among multitudes . glimmers of doubt ɪ had tried to abandon overwhelming . with each step haunted by routes not taken . choices split me into fragments . striving to fulfill every outcome . shattering these facets until ɪ can't locate myself

you're trying to realize too much the nightengale sighs *flow with the present . don't resist it*

aligning myself with the constellations . ɪ focus on locomotion . proceeding unsteadily yet gaining traction . until veiled thoughts are just an abstraction . feeling for what is tangible . faces peer out at me through portals of glass . apparitions ɪ have no control over . shuttered from inside . the camera lens impressions hide behind *they are prisoners as well* the nightengale laments

gradually we climb up the incline . out of limbo into the vista . piano keys forming steps . to the tune of a melody vaguely familiar . the pattern of it chiming before us forever . with dusk settling in a panoramic view . haloes floating at the borders of a city vaguely familiar

at the summit clouds begin to descend . hanging low when we approach . cautiously along the spire . gargoyles crouched upon them wielding vast sails . riding the storm high as a nimbus . from discus raining their thunderbolts against the rock . sundry stones tumbling before us in flashes of yellow

i pilot helplessly . and it is all we can do to stay on course . lashing out at the gargoyles' heels . who grin inverted in the maelstrom . from ripples of fabric the nightengale produces an umbra . deflecting the torrent just enough to avoid impact . so both of us battle to the brink of destruction . hinges derailing off axis

don't shy away the nightengale shrieks at the apex . as we race over the edge . wheels skittering out from beneath us with a crash . lightning striking down in climax

we sail through the air . weather dispersed in our wake . as we enter the atmosphere . anchors fading away . atop the empyrean where angels take flight . every demon surpassed with a sprite . zephyrs clearing the way for epiphany

now that we're tetherless . fluttering among the heavens . the globe is spread out below us in a map of oceans and deserts and rivers . this persona returning the gaze . like a moth to a flame . magnetic bearing no weight . the both of us observing from outside

curious . as we speed over the moon . I turn to glance at the nightengale . reflective with a smile *we are one and the same*

just when we are about to peak . streaking toward the ground . with a burst of flames we are released from orbit . launching against outer space . for we have landed on a sunbeam . revolving in a ring around the universe . where we merge together as a phoenix . flying into the sun . for my sol is complete the void bathed in light

♯
E
5
B
B
0
7
◇

celestial

don't shy away from the light
but return its gaze dazzling bright
nothing here is meant to remain
together when the currents change
if we'll never be the same
then find me where i have your name
i'll meet you at the surface there

i love you like i gasp for air

♯
F
2
B
B
A
D

ethereal

i found you in the soft place
before consciousness
bathed in the coldest yellow i ever felt
so i knew this was real
you were light in my embrace
but you passed from it
leaving me feeling
that will never be mine

♯
F
4
F
7
E
D

preamble

they say the eyes are the windows to the sol

but all ı'm seein' is a glass room
with little cracks in it

ı know ı'm bound to crack up
ı know ı'm not in tune

but when ı rectify my instruments the strings snap
so ı snap out of it and start again

after a try or two ı find
the best view's out of my mind

so ı begin to wander it
ı get lost in stride to ponder it

at what cost might this delay me
will my credit repay me

so ı resolve to squander it
no use to spend any longer in't

but instead ı crush myself

so here I am . looking down at it

through my pen and out of it

my mind's become a spectator-sport
and I'm reading over it

I guess this means that I'm over it
or does it mean that I'm out of it

over and out

voyeur

the best part of this
is that i meet you at my best

not when i'm in search of something

i see you not as a means
of happiness

but for who you are

regard you rippling
as a river

always changing

transparent . but with depths i can't decide

blinding . glimmering

i hear you laughing . amongst fragments

you tell me you're afraid

at the reaches of myself
I find you cold and strange

we are not painted . framed
but more than anything

I love you

faggot

ı used to dream of affirmation
now ı ornament the conversation
ı used to burn for admiration
now ı confuse the relationship

eat my loins and feed the nation
built on glass anticipation
kiss my cheek for entertainment
crooked laughs on tv stations
ı would know and you have told
pet my head it's straw to gold
leash me up until ı'm sold
come and reap what ı have sowed

but when i reach your heaven's gates
i've paid their dues and tempered fate
i could never take the bait
i'll pray to dust my sol to take

i pray to dust my sol to take

𝄪
F
7
E
E
B
0

◇

citrus

there is a vagina inside of my penis

i would peel back the foreskin
and show you
but you would tell me that's gross

i do not feel gross

to feel myself in the spring
i stroke bananas
and spit cherry pits

to feel myself in the summer
i lick mangoes
and carve cantaloupes

to feel myself in the fall
i gut pumpkins raw
and milk coconuts

to feel myself in the winter
i seed tangerines
and squirt citrus

if you have any questions
then suck me

all nature is ripe when it feels right

♯
5
8
B
2
E
F

◇

weather

nobody is happy always
it cannot be obtained
but in the moment
happiness isn't destiny

a traveler might
admire the path

while feeling nothing

there are times when
our emotions seem wrong

laughter born from misery

there are days so bad
we can barely endure

nobody controls
the weather

but it passes
in glimpses
that are beautiful

acids

i am looking for a memory

to crawl into a little while

it doesn't have to be real

it had better not

it just has to be furnished

with bright nonsense

lucid visions

that burn neon acids

i can feel a pain behind my eyes

they squirm like broken glass
inside my brain

and when i turn my head
it rattles them around

i am watching television

early in the morning

when i haven't slept

i open and go numb

far too detached to die

♯
4
B
A
0
7
1

◇

medium

I am the phantast
a creature of lark and escape
flickering between dimensions in static
arriving to your window prismatic
I peer out behind the glass
a vivid fantasy
offering all that can be found
pixels forming the extent of imagination
I am here to captivate
so that upon return one may perceive
beyond the boundaries of themselves

what was apprehended in the mirror
might become something new
♯
4
B
A
0
7
1
◇

familiar

there are those you
already know
when you've met
as if never strangers
you're unable
to describe each other
yet it feels wrong to call
it's like trying to justify happiness
one would rather appreciate
you share yourself without sharing
and inevitably as the tide
are drawn together again
so there's no goodbyes
only hello

♯
F
9
D
4
F
8

blossom

you cannot grow . cannot shrink
in who has loved you
blushing won't change
the color of evening
nobody dies your death
or is birthed your birth
your love cannot suffer for you
or follow your dreams
we're all alone in ourselves
beauty flowering
you cannot grow . cannot shrink
in who has loved you

but in what you have loved

♯
E
4
8
A
F
9

amber

do i exist anywhere
other than inside your head

i can feel myself writhing
from under your gaze

struggling to maintain my more solid form

it almost feels
like you do this on purpose

but as you say
it's just me being narcissistic again

still i can feel
the words you expect me to speak
beat out before me like a song
and so with a sigh of relief
i utter them

there are times i forget
what they are

and the meaning changes
regardless of what I do

it seems I exist
in a very tight space
shrinking beneath it
and I can't stop

it's a small world
becoming known to you

♯
F
B
D
5
D
6
◇

transparence

i don't have an identity
i am just making it up as i go along
awakening somewhere i don't remember
inside someone i don't belong
maybe one day i will try to make sense
of these walls rotating around me
but for now i drift
knocking into things
for fear of letting them down in some way
people call out a name i don't recognize

i have grown rather detached from myself
it seems i am watching my life as a stranger

♯
8
B
9
D
B
7

haven

the suburbs are hazardous
the streets uniform . i am tangled
and clatter my way into a hearse
the rise of the sol is predicted . simulant
i lay in the grass from sheer fear of it
how to keep track of the names and addresses
constellations that spit fire
i am too opaque to avoid them
and in horrible moments curse
at being damaged
by opening cages
i do not know where to leave
the wood is too dark
without validation
the sky immense
but would turn me blue in a minute
if i stay
some house is bound to come knocking
flat on my face

eyes smeared across toast

𝄪
C
F
D
8
E
E
◇

nobody

i do not understand identity
all the variation of existence
and resigning yourself to a name
when the potentials infinite
as the light changes by its reflection
never settling for
less than multitudes
i am different endlessly
uncompromising i decide
one identity doesn't
invalidate another

♯
F
B
D
5
D
6

nomad

I am the spider
weaving across the sky
trying to capture the stars
and reclaim their light as my own
it is said the universe may expand forever
from the singularity where it came
everything billowing away into darkness
unless something intervenes
so I dangle by this thread
drawing on my surroundings
to ascend the atmosphere
and consume the night
until all that exists
is complete

♯
F
B
9
F
B
A

◇

menagerie

on the way to byron kankles' palace we pass through the valley of little envelope people . my they are just absurd . how they open . they gather there . in the middle of the plaza . and unfold themselves for the world to see . you could go up and read one of them if you wanted . and know all about nem . it is utterly ridiculous . i think one ought to leave something for their own experience . there's no real fascination otherwise

this gathering i am headed to has been the talk of the surrounding area for some time now . all the nobles are invited . for byron kankles is one of the most respected in the neighborhood . it is quite a way for me . over in pearl dark . but the byron is generous of course and will have me a fortnight . i have anticipated this event for so long that i am really quite immaculate . my chariot is sleek obsidian . and drawn by the finest crabs in the whole platoon . the driver is rather out of practice . all my own doing . but i couldn't possibly trust the reigns to anyone other than arlington . and the ride has been so smooth today you really

wouldn't know it . as for myself . my hair is parted back in eight knots . each of them fastened with a little hook . my lashes long . dancing shadows on the rim of my ocean eyes . one of them is deeper than the other . i have noticed . but if i swim my ebon pleasant one can hardly know it . the dress of the evening is crescent silk . rippling gently in mine own penumbra . i will keep my shadows .
for tonight

i am arrived . and what a beautiful venue it is . byron kankles has a glass palace . situated square on the highest mesa in glimmer country . one can already tell it has been updated . for you can practically see inside it . though the light refracts . for it has mirrors and windows bending dimension . it is almost maddening . if you're disposed to that . but the brilliance is subdued . soft . even in the bright of day . and it has such a marvelous view of the planets . you could practically reach out and take one like a peach . and the moons . you can hardly keep track of they cross over so often . visible now is teeto and mycus . one green and one blue . and they bathe the desert in a peculiar marine light

i feel a touch of nerves as i descend the carriage . it really has been such a while since i attended an event . but am not entirely out of practice . the urchins and I have some of the most interesting discussions though they are terribly bashful . I remember just the other day picking one up and holding nem to my ear . just to make out what ne had to say . I flash a puckered smile on my descent though there are few . I note . to see it . just some servants . four or five of them for I am rather early . but none of them I recognize

there is a carriage now arriving just behind . so when arlington has seen me off I stop to attend it . I have not seen it before . yet it reminds me of something . rather quaint but in a charming way . it is very square with faded bronze . in a sense that indicates taste more than neglect . there is intention all about it . one is given the impression it could drive them leagues and leagues without ever wearing out

the noble is escorted down . and is revealed to be an odd individual . not even faintly handsome though admirably well-kept . nir brow is very broad . and sleek with little expression . and ne wears a bronze nose . but . still what hair ne has is tousled well . and nir suit is a warm grey not unbecoming of nem . it is the kind of visage one might seek approval from . for the details are authoritative . I am glared at with tired iron eyes

hello emtess roth

hello klev caravel I reply

the klev and I have something of a history . not romantic . never once . and I cannot say I have ever wished it to be . but there is peculiar tension between us . almost understanding . and though we have arrived in different carriages I expect it isn't lost . ne doesn't bow . and neither do I . but there is something of a nod intended for me . which is like a smile . I receive it with a dazzle of the eyes . I am always cool . but play at warmth when I can

we mount the steps together up to the entrance . led by a robed lycan who perhaps I have seen . little is said . not even pleasantries for I am distracted . the doors yawn far from resolve . with an inflection I don't comprehend . I feel something like vertigo fluttering at my breast . I am darting . flickering already . the palace casting my likeness in every direction . scattered to where I could never retrieve it . there are no shadows here . but then there is something else . a flash of stripes sleek across myself . then vanished there is a tiger here . ı remember . the tiger percian . the byron keeps nem to maintain the garden . a hunter to devour pests . none talk of nem . ne is simply something one must cross . ı have swallowed panic so that it simmers just beneath the surface of myself . it rose so quickly ı was apt to catch it . the klev helps me . ne is rational . as well as something like a tiger . something real . to balance with the other nonsense . we are passing now . and there is air to breathe inside

there are five guests gathered in the hall before a fountain . and ı expect there will be several more . it is an open space with many plants . nothing untame . and they give off a healthy citrus scent . there are sundry ferns stretched about singing sweet music . a wistful ambience . and they are lined with tangelo . the stair carves left and right like passing ribs . other domains of the palace glimmer skeletal above . ı notice myself among them . all is faded emerald now . mycus passing behind teeto far beyond

byron kankles is the first to greet us . ne is truly an excellent host . gregarious without patronizing . attentive without assuming . there is a hint of restraint . ı note . in nir demeanor . a self-awareness . it is apparent now . ne is tawny and broad . woods smoothed over rugged skin . ne has feline eyes and ne is handsome

elcome . elcome . good tuh see uh nir voice is burnt chimney smoak . ne is wilder than I remember . but not less happy

of the other four only one I recognize . the arch amelia . we don't get along at all . it is not hatred . there is mutual respect . but we could do without the other's company . I have always felt nir distaste for me and it revolves when we're together

ello emtess ne smacks loudly . as if addressing an elephant . ne is curved and very red . nir skin caked pale from the neck . nir eyes dark

hello I am tepid

this is my whore governet ne nods to a scrawny visage on nir right . governet is dressed in black with tufts of white . paint smeared on nir expression

and this is sev cable byron kankles puts nir arm around the shoulder of a statuesque figure . rather flat . ne smiles as if ne has broken *ne is studying with me for the summer*

and I'*m fillis* says a gargoyle rather long and spindly . spectacles perched on nir nose for ornament *it's a pleasure* . I *am sure*

we wait around a while . fillis is the most talkative . but benevolent . much of nir conversation is thoughtful questions . ne is a historian who seems to know much of every subject . I'm taken to nem . we drink from the fountain . crystal babbling at the surface . there isn't fresher drink to be had . the arch amelia spends a lot of the time grinning to governet . as if conspiring . governet . it turns out . is a nice enough fellow . though rather timid . byron kankles speaks for sev cable who continues to grin daftly . and klev caravel . cynical as ever . is not in ill humour . it is all around satisfactory company

two others arrive . whom I have met many a time . the vacancy twins . they are a mystery to me . the rumour is they have a triplet . one who died at birth . they always attend every event . but never have a thing to say . nor do they seem to particularly enjoy conversation to begin with . and they always dress in yellow but never match . sometimes they will trade clothes . in the middle

of a party . as if it were a joke . their eyes are
like blades . their skin as grey as can be . I don't
swallow them

that's our party for the night the byron announces
*the wan brigade won't arrive til the morrow . but
not to worry . I have many a diversion planned for
the evening . let's have a tour shall we . governet has
yet to see the place*

we ascend the steps and an odd regret grabs hold
of me . I am caught in a moment like a lurch .
as if about to fall . I regain myself . but am seen
. klev caravel is looking straight at me . nir grey
eyes seem to pierce through . I smile and slither
together . ne will not forget this . I suppose

we enter the library first . byron kankles is a
pragmatic individual . not one for poetry or
fiction . and the library is ornamented in but
maps and skeletons and plants . there is the
faintest sound of mandolin somewhere . ne has
traveled far in life . learned many trades and been
exposed to much . nir catalogue consists primarily
of manuscripts on botany . geography . astronomy
. really any branch of the sciences in many
languages . in spite of nir objective nature the
byron has good taste . but we do not remain here

long . fillis has many commentary on this place and the byron know it will tire us if left rampant

next is the velvet room . a hesitant marvel to us all . and certainly the reason some of us attended . if not for the garden it would make this place famous . the byron has mannequins for every size and taste . all of them perfumed in many flavors . they practically humn . even . not to mention the accessories . costumes of every fit and color . beds to host parties of twelve if needed . but we do not linger here . it is better left for later on tonight

following is the mint baths . we just pass through . it is much too calming for the night . the candles rather eerie . their fingers spindle such brazen puppets . i almost wonder if they're mocking us . teeto has abandoned the sky leaving the glass tinted blue . the water drips indigo

the private quarters aren't much to mention . just a reprieve from the wonders of the palace . mine is fitted lavish . though not quite to my taste . what one wants in a situation such as this is someplace to relieve a headache . and what with this luster that glints around whenever i move and the tinkling sensation it's a wonder i'll ever get to sleep at all . they must think it resembles

the trench . but the byron is always thoughtful
. and I know accommodations have been made
to the best of nir understanding . arlington has
tucked my things away and this will have to do a
fortnight

now for the garden . beneath all artifice that is the
agenda . we have held our breath . we mill outside
the door for moments . silent . the byron takes a
musket from the wall . any sound rings clear . ne
fumbles with the lock . we enter like a storm

the garden is the crown jewel of the palace . that
cannot be denied upon entrance . though one's
feelings toward it vary . I cannot locate my own .
it takes up many levels . it is impossible to decide
how many . for it is fragmented with windows
as well as mirrors . it is like staring into a gem .
seeing yourself flicker across endless dimension . it
cannot be perceived entire . for every movement
paints a different picture . it is something one
cannot stand to question . I see now many gardens
. infinity of them . inseparable in every direction
. stairs that twirl repetition like the pattern
of a fabric . I see myself shattered in awe . the
shards withered as dust . there are paths crossing
themselves . statues of every being . even the
atmosphere . the waning moon deandra below .

winking violet . a flush of baths . the tiger hidden
. all of it there a moment . and then gone

the purpose of this place is simple . a wilderness
within society . a controlled and yet organic
environment . to inspire

we have entered on a path one at a time . for
the way is narrow . it went the byron then sev
cable then the arch amelia then governet then
klev caravel followed by myself then fillis then
the twins . i am filled with the familiar vertigo .
unsure of my step . it is strange . the feeling never
grips me outside the palace . i am not alone in
it . all of us are silent . even fillis . there is never
conversation in the garden . we are being led
down a row of sunflowers with buck teeth . all of
them bending and swaying as if they might bite
us any second . but they are daft up there . hardly
aware of anything at all

we turn right into a pumpkin patch . i have never
been this way . there are several gardeners with
jack-o-lantern heads stumbling upside-down
amongst their brethren . really not attending to
anything particular . i hear the byron greet them
quietly but they don't seem to notice . there is a
well in this chamber . three cats perched at the

rim of it

next we cross the passage of roses . it is strange . the paths connect differently each time I am given a tour . there are always new surprises . they are tall and dark pink . flickering bright and then dimn with their breathing . their stems are black . reptilian and thorned . and they are constantly squirming . I have heard that they favor the byron . getting jealous when ne brings visitors . I do not doubt it . for there is frustration about them

we get through unscathed and enter a pleasanter area . the lavendar woods are filled with bees the size of tennis . as fuzzy as can be and very kind . they made me a garland once . out of brambles and little petals . they brought it right over and I wore it round my neck to excite them . they are a little out of character today . fewer and sluggish . I wonder what happened . but it doesn't occur to ask . the byron never talks of the garden

the village of daffodils is my least favorite . they hate us for stepping between their houses . I can just feel it . they run about through the rows to and fro . peeping out windows and chattering in the most frightening voices . it is like singing the same shrill note incessant . they always carry with them teacups . but never have a thing in them to drink . i am grateful when we've passed . lucky i didn't step on something

we are climbing stairs now . i am focused on my footfalls . the rail clutched . klev caravel in mine eye . to glance in an other direction is like to throw myself out in the abyss . it is dimn . not a moon in the sky . just a hint of orange upon the complexion . i can feel the garden spiral beneath me in unfathomable scope . unraveling from my control . i cannot reconcile this infinity of my mind . no matter i try

we have ascended the pond and it is filled with smoak . an odd favorite of mine . more staid than elsewhere . reality but a hazy memory . the orange light peers from within . just across the water . ne is getting bigger . we stand in an arc at the brink of nem . pacing toward us . ne is the tiger percian . each pale step rippling casually at the mirror . ne glows dimn . but is bright by comparison . nir stripes purest shadow . ne has come to retrieve something . but what . we get down on our knees in prayer . for ne is stalking among us . the water hesitant to display nir movement as we plea to be chosen . there is no depth beyond the surface . only what is reflected . in final response nir head

bows selection . firmly . and with such grace nir
jaws baptizing the crown of klev caravel until
blood runs like ripen fruit from nir temple . and .
as graciously as ne came . the tiger percian returns
over the horizon . the twitching body of the klev
dangled at nir wrist

our eyes filled with tears . all traces of the tiger
fade from the heavens . it is unknown how
long we remain . but certain we mustn't linger .
nebulous . yet with conviction we gather ourselves
and descend

we banquet out in the court . cathandra . the wild
moon is out . and we feast beneath nir yellow eye
. it is a hot night . many servants to attend us .
bringing in plates upon platters of most delectable
refreshment . there is fruit that's spouting blood .
warm bread thickening nuts . meat that practically
breathes it is so fresh . there are fine soups
iridescent . wine fermented from ground ruby .
wooden chocolate that fills the air with incense
. vegetable fountaining sea foam . the twins are
stripped naked . running like little fools through
the clover patch . fillis is positively swelling with
tales . rivers of tears glisten nir viola . byron
kankles simply cannot keep nir hands off sev cable
. modest as ne feigns to be . and the arch amelia is

at a fight with governet . who is lying palms down
in the grass . 1 myself am filled with the strangest
. most horrible winking laughter . so fierce 1 fear 1
may away

there is a particular game that we play upon
nights such as these . when the senses are lulled
into a kind of stupour . croquet . there are several
targets of varying sizes and color situated among
us on the court . all of them round and buoyant
. each is worth a number of points . one takes a
tonic . mounts the tower . and then flings nemself
from the window . the aim being to spring from
one target to the next using the tonic as a relaxant
. and earn as many points possible . 1 must say as
an ocean dweller 1 am rather good at it . though
it is surely the most dreadful diversion . just last
year susan susan shattered in so many fragments
ne was never recovered . not fully . parts of nir jaw
scattered about here to this day

we are going to play it

we draw fates from the basin . and 1 of course
have selected the red stone . we all laugh and 1 roll
my eyes and begin the ascent . it is better gotten
over with . 1 reach the window and have a long
look down . it is strange . all the vertigo is gone

. the moon wanes so I remove the top from the tonic and drink a fifth . then . with a short laugh I throw myself out in the night

♯
D
9
C
A
D
B
◇

wayward

they
seem to think
you don't know
you're beyond
recognition
but in the way
that they frown
it's apparent
that you
with your sonorous face
and your crooked voice
become quite the clown
when you say
something
that isn't true
rather than face a bored crowd

so now
all your tickets have sold
all the stands gone
so you go
and pack up your things
to move on to a town

where your tricks
might last
a bit longer

♯
E
B
9
3
B
3

uncanny

the world will devour me
for i do not understand it
it is merely biding its time
to savour the chase
once it has given me a name
like a great snake
it will lure me into its folds
for the sake of justice
it cracks me open
a yolk for the mouths
of its hungry audience
the details change
so covertly we don't notice
but the theme remains
we fight in the name of peace
we kill for fun

♯
9
3
6
C
5
D
◇

mannequin

i am removed from the tongue
that saturates skin
it salivates and i don't
i am displaced here
a mannequin hollow and stiff
but apparent enough you can draw
whatever expression you want
do you like meat
here . take this with you
i'll pack it in my fucking placenta
an alien egg
found in the walls of a satellite
that defied the expectations of your computer
won't you turn me off
like an animatron . far too uncanny
i have carried a plague over the stars
to avenge all extinction humanity wrought
on whatever reminds them

they are doomed

♯
F
F
E
7
D
3
◇

salve

what am I supposed to do with all of this furniture

it's hideous-green . almost fuchsia

and it sags and sways
with my grilled cheese-breath

I am a bright rash

if these walls ever faded
I would glow in the dimness

though it is far too humid to ever get dark

why did I ever invest in myself
I can't make the payments

and this property has been flooded so long
there is nothing to do with it

the fluids I wade in up to my waist
are the same that foamed
from my mouth as an infant

my ankles swell
forests grow from the largesse chicken-feet

and the fleas won't go
they eat the sweet crust of my head

I salt it myself
I feel sorry for them

we've both of us nowhere to swim to

and there's nothing to do
with all of the grogginess but slop it around

being far too dirty to clean a thing

I am nothing but a sore red thumb
pulsing impatient for rusted amputation

♯
F
F
6
8
4
6

validation

nothing that exists is worthless

for you are part of a whole

letting go of the need to justify your existence

to others . to yourself

no longer being defined by purpose

and having this experience

for the discovery of it

is as close as one can come to freedom

if not freedom itself

JF
B
3
7
B
5
5

palms

i look for freedom
on the back of my hands

i look for freedom
at the roadside

i look for freedom
gleaming in the twigs

i look for freedom
in distant galaxies
and the prospects they hold

i look for freedom
from my memory

i look for freedom
on the horizon

i look for freedom
reflected in the moon

I look for freedom
of interpretation

I look for freedom
in others

but never in myself

I am not that fool

0
0
0
B
4
A

time

for all the presents past

and all the eras gone

for all the stars burned out

and all the journies end

for all the reach of space

and whatevers there

1 am here

this moment's mine

♯
4
0
2
7
0
D

divinity

answer your
prayers

♯
E
F
E
F
E
F

gloaming

you are the pen burning a hole
right into my pocket

desperation of the sol
how am I to stop it

you are the reason I rise and then
fall back into my bed

you're every single thought
that runs against my head

they say that when you're lost
go looking for a light

but you are all I've got
you are my starlight

and if I were to drown tonight
you'd be the only end in sight

second star and to the right

but if I'm ever to truly rest
I've got to get you off my chest

I know I have to face you now
but I've no one to show me how

smoak

you love it
the bones in your marrow
the city etched out before

you . a map

the palms of your hands an
internal clock
you get up
at three o'clock
the smell of rain
you can't sleep
something came to you
in a dream
you won't remember
caffeine tangles your head

superstition
the air is fresh
you step out
a hint of smoak
catches your throat

the familiar death
you drive

and don't think of music
cause the lights bathe you

in a glow

so melo
you hope to crash
you have waited so long
for something terrible
to happen

♯
F
2
B
2
7
E

asleep

i think i love you better blind
with the tatter on your shores
and the ashes in your skies
we were met in garbage times
with towers overhead
and glitter on my lips
i took the knife out of your back
and laid it in your chest
confessed to seeing all
and saying nothing
you built my dreams and
left them in my head
i mourned your wounds
but never bled
let us put to rest instead

♯
C
7
9
9
C
5

tartarus

it must be something about oblivion
that gets me squirming in the mire
i know it's there when i begin to sink
though i've never reached the bottom
these rivers are soiled by what they carry ashore
spiteful veins turned green with envy
pleading amputation from a body
i must crawl so far i don't need legs

i must grow so large that
blood means nothing

♯
C
9
C
9
7
D

myopia

nobody asked to exist
we are all living a conditional experience
piloting a body our own
and dying alone . not omniscient
this ignorance creates conflict
there are mistakes beyond redemption
change does not absolve what has been inflicted
and oftens empathy reveals that justice is deserved
there has to be consequences for people's actions
to keep them from repeating
but no matter how we diverge
it is import to understand one another

to find solutions where they are

♯
A
9
E
0
9
9

◇

entropy

reality isn't solid enough
I tried to observe it
yet it slips through my fingertips
pricked as I thread what's been broken
with all I perceive as a fabric
still I couldn't fathom it
the evidence lost
of this pattern
unraveling the

universe

♯
4
9
3
0
6
3

panorama

no system is omniscient
or can be truly objective
therefore to learn one must
venture beyond paradigm itself
when viewed from the outside
only then can structure be understood
how it came about . its bias and motivations
so that it can be applied as a framework
when needed
to help shape your understanding
without limiting it
for the more your mind remains open
the more you see everything

♯
A
A
8
7
7
B

apocalypse

the oceans are stacked
in towers so tall
but i draw lines in the sand
constellations
so small
that
i'm
almost
convinced
that
they're
real

♯
A
A
8
3
8
3
◇

change

we
are
born
of
balance
and
depend
on
it

♯
8
C
A
D
7
2

evolution

is it wrong to find beauty in madness

i think i thrive in the contrast

between the self and the self

i think i need the extremes

monotony bores me

i don't want to tread for the sake of it

i am bred of

victory and defeat

divinity won't save me

my only hope is to remain curious

♯
5
B
4
1
5
2

◇

harrow

if we are to live

it might as well be to see the end

we can finally breathe

knowing we are breathing for the breath

not continuance

we are at our best

beyond the edge

fear nothing

♯
2
C
3
A
3
1
◇

origin

your consciousness

is the surface
of eternity

beneath lies
singularity
where all things
converge

into a star

♯
8
7
A
A
8
F

dwell

have you faded

it began as a wish cast vaguely from my thoughts
. when I saw the comet course over the mountain
. that perhaps there was something beyond
this perception . I had long accepted the scope
of my existence . so from its inception the
idea progressed insidiously . and by the time I
recognized what was happening there was nothing
to be done about it

things began to lose their vitality . I noticed it first
during harvest . when the fruit became devoid of
flavor . the texture of ash in my throat . like trying
to recover a memory . and I was then unable to
smell the smoak from the chimney . just a catch
in my breath . opposite suffocation . even my
blood . cut at the root ran transparent . it was easy
for a while to dismiss as a change of season . the
gloaming had begun after all . and I knew every
figment of the valley regardless . but then others
were concerned . their eyes unfocused upon me .
they told me I appeared waxen . my voice quiet .

and they became blurred as if apparitions

i was taken to the herbalist . the physician . the alchemist . numbed by their hands and measured as vapour . but none of them offered any decisive conclusion . for the evidence dispersed in their grasp . seeming to transcend nature . yet there were whispers of someone who ventured beyond logical practice . into intuitive measures that could not be explained . given the state of my condition i was finally admitted to the praecantrix . who told me i needed to leave

i had been drawn . ne said . almost as soon as i entered . beyond this reality . i needed to journie past the end of the world . or else fade from existence entirely

incredulous as this was to believe . there weren't other solutions . i read everything in the library . arranging the words in all possible answer . but the village was so dimn i could hardly make anything out . shadows of those i knew flickered about me upset but i could no longer hear them . finally in the night . when the stars were no paler than during the day . i resolved to go . there was simply nothing left for me here

at the edge of the valley lies a mountain . where
the comet disappeared . when one climbs it . void
meets them on the other side . just a country of
blank . throughout history few have ventured
into it . and none of them returned . it is strange
i rarely regarded it . an object too abstract for
consideration . only now it seems to be my final
tether to this realm . i feather up the ridge . it is
hollow . and i am so light i can practically drift to
the top . there is little sadness in my departure .
when reality fades it hardly feels real . after all

i ascend the summit . and for the first time in
my life look past it . there is just a white space .
without hint of depth or of shadow . only now
i'm certain that something is there

i cross over the boundary . and do not fall but
merely tread . what remains of my body seeming
to blaze a path through the abyss . there is solace
in the endeavor . defining a will of my own . i do
not look back but can feel the world recede . there
is something like truth in emptiness . as if matter
were but a distraction . from an eternity . i feel
powerful . for once able to move with conviction
. toward a destination . and whether it is the
contrast my stride seems significant

ı travel a while that cannot be measured .
there is nothing to reference it with . just my
body migration and desolate . notions of space
harrowing my thoughts . memories linger with
little purpose . as if they belong to somebody else
. yet ı maintain the sense of progress . becoming
either stronger or confident . so after an age and a
moment have passed . when ı notice the fountain
. it might as well be the first thing to ever happen

ne is a statue . celestial from a distance . a mirage
too alluring to question . more distinct than
reality . for ne is all that exists . directing my
course to nem . ı could turn away and still be
drawn . by an angel winged . nir tears streaming
into the basin over which ne hovers . sparkling
. yet there is nothing brilliant nor shrouded
about nem . but peculiar certainty . as if ne were
engraved upon the world . the rest of us here to
admire it

there is no signal when ı near . justifying this
visitation . no form of instruction or purpose .
just the surface . flowing in perfect harmony .
ı creep to the brim of it . and peer in . past my
reflection . with a glimpse ı am reminded . of
everything

there is a wish . cast to the bottom . revealing a
pattern . for which there is no description . not
unlike a spiral arcing into itself . the tears that
have been cried are not water . but the fabric of
existence . the spectrum of reality . and colors
i had never before fathomed . creation itself
displayed before me in clarity . every possibility
deconstructed into quintessence . from which
anything imaginable may be conceived . the
universe a medium for something infinitely
simpler . and entire

upon awakening the strangest is the sense of it
being there all along . lingering in the back of
my mind . i was just too distracted by entropy to
notice . what it gravitates around . dreams that
seemed abstract are now absolute . constellations
revealed in the chaos . thoughtless i mount the
ledge . all fear dispelled at the source . but a limb
to the body . i reach past the surface . delving
through this dimension . to what lies beyond it .
the fountain is ripples . clear to the bottom . all i
must do is enter my gaze

shattering the mirror i am submerged . all
of infinity swirling around me in fractals of
perception . suspended in perfect balance . both
sinking and swimming i descend the stair . caught

by a maelstrom toward the bottom . from which
the comet is the lasting center . my prayer that
this may have a purpose . if only I can discover it .
thrashing against the capricious tide . the fountain
subsides . and I am immersed without tether .
my body alone in the vortex . scattered before me
in fragments . for I egress no closer to resolution
. the pattern repeating nowhere . the answer is
always just out of grasp . to exist is a paradox .
from which there is no escape

I drift in the current endlessly . pulsing until
I no longer struggle against it . for I cannot
comprehend why I am here . or the meaning of
that question . unable to conceive an alternative .
just an echo growing fainter to where it is lost in
translation . and the sense of something forgotten
. I do not know whether I drown . or am simply
absorbed . so by the time I recognize I have
vanished . I am nothing but a void

there is consciousness . in the abyss . from I
don't know where . or perhaps this is my mind
. descending from a body unknown . sensory
notions of light . sound . touch . taste . smell .
space . time . the astralis forming my will in a
halo . for I am all that can happen . cast from a
comet and melded into a diamond . realized by

every facet . and for what . to become absorbed
is to embody . within emptiness lies possibility .
yet there is something glaring behind it . a wish to
be granted . that i am the answer . to spiral is to
revolve . to shrink . to enter . i am born . beyond
reality

if this transmission reaches you . find comfort in
knowing . there will always be that beyond what
you understand

F
F
F
2
F
6

entity

sometimes I see
everything
staring in the mirror
at what lurks behind it
eternity returns my gaze

we are but a mask
the night wears

⧣
1
1
0
0
5
1
◇

night

ɪ want to shed existence
in the middle of a breath

more sudden than ɪ came

so that the night might wonder
what the exhalation would have been

a final kiss shared with myself

♯
1
A
1
F
3
D

chariot

it is such a far way to the ground

I love it up here but am sure to burn out

I am not afraid enough of these things

I look to the galaxies and relate to them

but am fragile

this body is not housed for my desire

♯
6
9
1
C
0
0
◇

abyss

this is how we fall forever
nature didn't do this . it is balanced
we crossed the edge
to spite ourselves
there is power at
the endless bottom
we came to understand
that falling is the same as flight
we are winged angels
sailing into the sun
knowing that our rage will
yield in fiery rapture

♯
9
1
3
B
5
5

dusk

this won't last forever
but when we're together
it's solace I would never question
your breath is cast from my lungs . a spell
consciousness formed in what we don't articulate
the planets revolve slower as we trace their motion
mistakes hang useless where they aren't regarded
there's nothing to harvest
we came to watch the sun set
it perpetuates beyond the haze of our world
vermilion as a cataract
we are fuel to be consumed
both selves melded into one
I'm almost certain
I belong with you

♯
A
F
6
1
3
F

wisteria

there will come a day
when you will
push them all away
and then they'll
stay gone
what a surprise
that the world doesn't
revolve around you
you always had to have
it on your terms
you'll come down from
whatever mountain
you're hiding in
and nothing will be
waiting for you

♯
A
7
D
6
C
9

bathe

i feel my desires erect
the moon doesn't seem very far
shining over all i perceive
silver coins shower in her branches
i cast them from my net
too desperate to bother with pockets
they would wrangle themselves into fish
lost in the vastness
i think i prefer to admire the possibilities
than swim after them
they aren't mine to decide
though i am glad to receive
i continue this journie on the river
hearing their song in the distance
we are apart
but everything that

♯
9
flows returns
1
A
F
B
7

◇

destiny

there is music
that was meant to happen
when you first discover it
you feel as if you have before
not that it resembles what has come
but has a spirit entire
it isn't creation

it's eternity

♯
8
B
F
2
D
E

phenomena

what determines the quality of art

the opinion of critics are fickle . and the narrative of acclamation changes all the time . some are in search of subtlety . others boldness . evolving with the current fashion . but never the same thing . for it is subjective . many works that are renowned today were alien upon release . these are often the most influential . opening the mind to new ideas

it can be concluded . then . that the best art is not concerned with whether it is loved or hated . famous or obscure . it doesn't slave to rigid structure . doesn't try and compromise . but has an identity all its own . a sense of purpose . and fulfills its full potential

great art defines itself

♯
E
8
A
7
E
6

art

is
finding beauty
in entropy
deciphering meaning
from chaos
bridging possibility
with reality
discovering eternity
in transience

♯
A
7
D
6
C
9

imagination

ɪ'm more interested in
possibilities than reality

reality is fixed . and often feels arbitrary

there are only so many paths
you can take as yourself

whereas art is limitless

ɪ will never realize all that ɪ want in this life

but the transmission of ideas

has unlimited potential

♯
F
2
D
3
E
C

wisdom

wisdom is languorous and self-satisfied
we become so blinded by what we know
that we fail to recognize what is
let us not hold the future hostage
with antiquity
but embrace reality
remaining present as it evolves
it is good to learn from history
and celebrate our legacy

but not prevent change

♯
B
B
C
A
F
9

intuition

there is truth unspoken
for being inarticulate
does not make it unreal
the moon herself understood
but not what she manifests from
there is something beyond
what we comprehend
a vision to worship
the unknown as known
to understand what is there
the pattern unravelling at our touch

but just because it is discovered
doesn't mean it's not magic

♯
A
7
D
6
C
9

astralis

ı like to express myself
sometimes as a tree . often as fruit
dimly aware of my roots
my light is taken . a confused lantern . directed
to reveal what ı am
ı like to observe
a faraway sol
scattered in night
lest ı forget
in the throb between spaces
and lash out in terror
of the unknown
so that ı might fall in love over again
it is a good feeling
awareness
it is enough
it is enough
4
A
0
0
F
F

◇

phantasmagoria

it is suffocating
how impending death
certain destruction
empires fall
none remain
life is transience
but we burn
whether it consumes us we're brilliant
the night is dancing
a phantasm of color
harrowingly vague
if we cannot but exist
why not dance along

♯
3
8
2
9
4
7
◇

moth

there is the concept of the sol
a flame of you that is eternal
but to exist at all
is that not infinite
the cosmos bright
merely shifts
nothing never had from something
to burn
is to burn
always

♯
E
7
C
A
B
9

transcendence

I am looking out the window now . it is dark in this room . and the window gloams dimly from the table . I wonder at touching it . it is in silence . but it is gloaming so that means that somebody is calling . it is either mom or it's mama . or maybe both of them on both of the windows . I don't know many others . I am not going to answer . I should break the window away but I'm not going to do it just yet . I have to feel good about things before doing them . and I don't . I'm a bit cramped . now . I like the dimness in here but not as much as I get bored of the same place . it's less boring than home . though . there I have to be solid for everyone . here I have the freedom of being more of a liquid . filling whatever space I spill into . but almost never being caught . yet I am tired of this dimness . I have to get out of here

so I go around and check the faucet . the window . the face and the door . and I spill out into the city daytime . it's a little bit bright . but not very hot yet . and I am glad for the sunlight . right now . there are many homosapiens here . I both like it and dislike it . I don't like bumping into someone . which is difficult not to do . but they are all very interesting to look at . there are so many faces that are blotted in reds and blues and oranges and green and yellow and purple and in shades of grey . they are very pretty . too . all of them have so many heights and angles and brushes . all of them very strang in their way but that is really the greatest part . everything comes from a different world of its own and for that nothing is very boring

everybody has a window with them . they wander along . drawing it in so many different directions . I do not blame them . the windows can be very interesting . but I didn't take mine with me today . sometimes it clamps too hard around my thoughts and I have to give it away . there are many buildings here . they breathe . and are mostly green . I get a little bit of nervousness when I'm around them . so much is spilling from them . and they sway . all of them gently in little patterns that I cannot trace after . soon I find myself spinning as well . but not in their ways . sometimes I'm sure I will step too hard . while all of the windows are spinning . and take off from the ground towards outer-space . the sky is so pretty here . no clouds today . but i'd be sure to smack into something

smack there is a voice now . sharper from the other crowd . thicker than all of them have . it is blaring at me

sor it says . halting me into my place . i feel buggish . twitching from the other bodies . my movements stick like syrup . there is a homosapien . i look . standing in a door . nir window bounding in front of nem . it has chaos regions about it . ne is directing me . ne is a grey color . nir hair and skin submerged in shades of blue . i cannot see eyes very well . they keep on dancing very watery from varied windows *youer look vereh much laek merh frien geofrh . mayb' a liddle old*

o my voice sounds strange . i am confused . i try to dance the way nir window does but it is garbled . it doesn't translate well to me

nir eyes look on me now . the windows for a moment lifted . i feel for some time since very afraid . it is a strange emotion to be seen such as that . when someone looks at you closely . you are a reptile . your pupils shrink . and something

very old that isn't you peers from without . it is
something that's hard to accept

it's not bad ne goes on *geofrh clens up real noice
from taim tuh taim . but* I *hafta go sire . goobye* and
with that ne is snuffed up beyond the door . just a
reptile left looking within . it shudders . there are
many homosapiens surround it . chittering . and
so it shuffles its way back among them

I have noticed something of late . I don't look
like everyone else . not anymore . I don't think
I translate as well as I used to . all of them swim
in blues . ripples . but I have more yellows than
that . it is a bright yellow . almost green . it
tingles the way that you spin when you have spun
for too long and now the world is gross . I am
a fever . I noticed it at home . too . but I never
thought about it much until this place . all of the
homosapiens here swing . swing in endless circles
that don't ever stop . it makes me sick . I am not
as sharp as that

ah . I have gone far . there is a dim vibrance . very
translucent and reflective . drifting on the wall .
it is a ufo . coming over the hillside with a little
town sleeping below . it is pulsing . with the title
stargazer framed in nostalgia neon . I go along the

wall . but the other windows are blurry to me . i am only appealing to *stargazer*

i seem to have believed in fate . i check the numbers and stargazer is on in ten minutes . the shadows aren't very much anymore . and there will be less of them in an hour's time . i seem to have come to the very right place

with my ticket i enter . and it is very much cooler . i didn't seem to notice how dry i was until now . there are homosapiens in here too . a little less smoothed with the dimness . but i can move around without getting in their way . my mouth keeps getting stuck on itself . so i purchase a cola to loosen it up . and wander into the theatre

everybody is here . i didn't know they were all free today . it is very hard to see there are so many windows dancing . my seat is very bad . but it is on the wall so at least i can watch around me . i focus very hard . but the windows blink . and i seem to have stepped on somebody's foot on the way there *ah* i hear . i feel really terrible . i don't say anything in response because i haven't used my voice much today and so i am scared of what it might sound like . ne doesn't come after me . though . i get in my seat and am tucked away

safe . ne is some homosapiens away and if ne had
wanted ne would've come after by now . a weird
sadness comes over me . why do i always take up
so much space . it is really just a problem of mine
. i wish i had a shorter body . one to use much
more quietly . but we can't change these things

there are commercials now . i really don't bother
them in my sadness . it is nice when things
happen short sometimes . because then they don't
stop being fun . none of them this time around
are very interesting to me . but the colors are
bright . and all of them done very differently .
there is one with lots of gunshot-sounds . it is
strange . that gunshots don't mean anything in a
window

the commercials are finished . and pretty much
everyone has put their windows away . i do not
remember what sadness is like . it is just a big
window here and all of our bodies are pretty
sloppy compared to it . the colors are dimn . but
because so i notice them more . so that when they
brighten they spread all around me . i am bobbing
. now . most all of us are bobbing . generally
drawn in to the window . i do not hear breathing
. the colors have swept into us . i am not myself .
the screen reads stargazer

I am a boy named fray who lives in a small town . I have lived there for my entire life . I am good-looking with everything going for me . but I am lonely and eighteen years old . I do not know what to do with my self . I have recently graduated from school at the top of my class but it feels like something is missing . so I have taken time off to work and figure things out . I go for drives by myself and listen to lots of acoustic-rock ballads . thinking wistfully of the past . it is the future I regret

one day . a girl friend comes to visit . we were girl friend and boy friend the year before . when I used to play on the varsity sports-team . but she went away and I stayed . it was sad without her . but now it is even sad with her . she hasn't changed very much . but I feel heavy with what has passed . I can tell she feels sorry for me and it makes me very pathetic . the evening ends and we will not be together

I go and sit out on the roof by my self . when it is over . like I always used to . the nightscape is very beautiful to-night . almost better than I ever saw it . I see a star in the distance and wish for an answer . to how I will never regret the future any longer .

the star gets bigger . it is movements . it is coming towards me . it is a ufo . i am abduct. ed

they tell me about myself . the things i don't know . and the truth . the aliens do . they say that a long time ago the universe lost something . and so life was created to find it . at the end of everything is where something went missing . they say that my genetic code is a map . a map to solving the mystery . i am chosen

i am very confused in my head . and i am angry . the aliens are ugly to look at and i am trying to be close-minded . we are travelling very fast . and everyone i know from my planet will be dead soon . but the hard part is that i'm excited . it is strange . but i am uncertain i could have lived out my life on the earth and been happy

we go on lots of adventures together . me and the aliens do . there are many planets with big waterfalls and mean storms and the yellow places . in some situations i save them from harm and in others they save me . i have warmed up to them . they are no longer so ugly now that i understand

the end

the colors fade to static and I am confused . I am like swimming in a fog of my mind . but I do not know whose it is . it is my self . the credits are going . now . and there are windows passed around . I wonder that there must've been some mistake . the movie ended shorter than it should have . I wonder if there is a part-two . I am frustrating because I liked the movie but I don't have a satisfied feeling after . they never did get to the end of the universe . they never did solve the mystery . I don't feel like getting up . now

it is strange . the colors in the window were prettier than in real life . but there weren't any more or less of them . and the voices . too . they were chatter clearer . even the aliens I could understand . it is difficult for me to return from that feeling . I am more nostalgic for it than my own self . it seems to me that . when framed . life is better . it goes on in a better way . even when it's bad . or maybe it really was a better world . in there

but here . this place that I live . there are aliens too . it is said that the universe goes on for for ever . so there has got to be . I wonder about where they are

everyone has left the theatre except for me and a
friendship of homosapiens . they are a row or two
behind me . I can listen to them talking

*ver art form . yerh . I laik et because et verh how laif
is . no answer . buddaih think is taim to goh . I em
ver . hunger*

I cannot tell the voices apart . they are strange to
me . but I know that they are talking about the
movie . as they make their way down the steps
I see three bodies in the windows . it is strange .
they resemble the homosapien from the door .
swimming blues . they are slender and quick . I
follow on after them . I cannot help it . they seem
to have interesting things to say and I don't want
to be alone . right now

I follow them into the street . and they don't seem
to mind noticing . it is bright . the sun is less high
than it was earlier . but my eyes seem to bleed on
the concrete . it really bothers me and I can't blink
enough . there are more homosapiens than there
were before . and it is difficult for me to trail the
friendship without seeming like a weirdo . a shirt
and some shoes that's dancing windows keeps on
getting in the way . and it is frustrating business
. I can only catch glimpses of their conversation

. but I hear fray and the wasp so I know they are talking about stargazer still . there is something to have learned from them . they do not seem dissatisfied with the film itself so maybe if I keep listening I won't be dissatisfied . either . I want to understand . it is really very important to me

they have entered a building and it is frustrating . we have gone a ways but I have heard liddle . the building calls itself twenty-four hour breakfast . and I have seen it before . it has big windows they are always orange . I am suddenly very hungry . I just realized . I realize that I haven't eaten for some time . I believe when I have eaten I will be hungrier . in fact . I cannot remember the last time I ate some thing . it was yesterday . sometime

I follow them in . after leaving some minutes to not be strange . and there are very few homosapiens inside . it is an odd time of day to eat some thing . I can see the friendship in a corner . but the host is blocked . ne catches me with little hook and is trying to seat me in the wrong way . it is very flustering . I am like frozen in place *it is lighter over there* something says . but it is not the truth . there are eyes all over me . like spiders . I am twitching now . not following any way . I want to just leave but that is very

conspicuous

sire . sire a voice slams me from across the cage
. it is clearly mine . from one of the friendship .
I cannot tell which . they are just staring . now
. three little bulbs . all of the windows lifted .
there is not a space in which I hide . I am seen
from behind . I can feel others not belonging to
the voices . all of them foreign and different .
somewhere very high . somewhere I don't belong
. they have thoughts of their own . things I don't
understand . I am like slipped at the edge of their
irises . buried to fall for for ever

*sire . you can . t keep on follerh us . iss been much is
way . is been so lon . as been too*

I am backed away . mumbling things that do not
feel like the thoughts I have said . I cannot hear
them . it is gone . it passes through garbled water
. I have lingered here for too long . there has to
be an escape . I am like spilt away through the
door from twenty-four hour breakfast . and the
openness has a big mouth . there are like snatches
now . snatches of music . of faces bleached white
by the sun . flickering past . they are moving
against me . I am tossed . resisting the current .
the tide is so strong and I am so small . I cannot

move in a staid way . canno t breathe . the air is stifled . everything is like soggy draining all of the air

ahguhahuh I spring into the street . the cars are screaming . but it doesn't matter . they cannot glimpse me too long . a moments' terrible I am the other side . secured back to my feet . there are wanderings here too . that have noticed me . but much fewer . I dart into a snaky path away from the open space . there are no bodies . here I am like running . now . darting so fast and knowing my feet very well . the cola is here but that is all right because I know a zig-zag back to this place I am staying . I have like calmed down from being so frustrated that now I am calmed . I am like simmering . simpering . but I will not cool off . now . I can handle what is needed for a little while

I have reached an impasse . I am at the corner that leads you to the corner where this window I am staying in is . but the way is blocked . there is a pack of homosapiens . very wild and natural . surround something . I do not want them to bother me . they all of them have windows out . but I have to pee and can go noplace else . I move soft in my approach . all of them are stared away down at something . they are throwing comments

themselves but i do not understand them . i see a
figure through the blues . buried in the ground . it
is wet and pale and fat . its head sunk into vomit
. its chin is like nothing . gopher teeth . it cannot
breathe in that way . i have waded amongst them .
they are . filming . it

wettness dropples on concrete . my legs can sting .
my pants rubber . salty . i am like waiting for turn
around . i keep peeing . it is a conscious depth of
my mind . can't they smell me . i smell my self

one of them has turnt around and is close .
through nir window eyes branded like flames
of hell fire . i look away . they still are . it is
confusing . it is terror . it is disgust . ed

by me

i seem to have been very long . cluttering on my
backwards palms from the group and blinking
windows . it is like my arms might scatter me
broken along . my penis chafes my salty pants and
i do not bother about such things . now i am like
blind to the world and grow blind-ler . i have to
hide away before i am nothing-ness

ahhh i am struck by lightning and crunched in

the ground . my head is like maggots strucked in the twigs . and I can't squirm around gather it . everything pulsating red . everything ringing and turning . my arms clenched like dead spiders' carcusses . my spine curled in a clenched fist . I am skittered back onto my-self because ther is not anything left to ride . there is no up nor down and I am blinked by a bike and nir biker all crackling pop sideways . a face is terror . ised

arse you okay . I'm verrhu sorrum

mm my mouth is in stitches slopping . my glass pieces cut teeth . it is like broken marbles inside my mouth . I drip slobber at my lips that is blood . I am skittered up on the door and in places . lucky and fumble a key from the sand in my clothes . I am drippling and droppling my self all over pale everything . I am sniffed up by a bloody nose knife in the brain and . have escaped

I have cum down the hall and bled back to this room that is locked away from the other world . it is good I know the secret way . though I am trapped in this prison . now I am crawled into this bed and alone . the window gloams dimnly from the table . I am like fossilized to this bed and wonder if life stops . I am not tired but do not think until I have passed a . way

I wake up to the call . I do not know I have slept
. but I was not awake this time . the window
gloams from the table . I hurry up and change
into something fresh because I cannot be wearing
mypee to the alien greeting . I do not know what
they smell like . but I am curious to . know I
have changed in my clothes and am clamber out
onto the window-still . the night is like a window
hung upside- down . its breath is cool air . like
something forgotten . I always seemed to have
known I would get the call . it is like in my acids .
I need to have meant something . why else would
I have krept awake for this long . the city lights are
twinkling below me . but stayed . they do not run
too fast for me . there are better lights of mine . it
doesn . t matter if the concrete scrapes my palms
because I have something else . I have reached
these moments and am ready . there is nothing
even to hold on to . I can see the ufo winking not
far off and so I know its secrets . the secret that
it's time to go . h I am like running now . I do
not need to feel my self although I do . the edges
passed away and . I am taking off from the ground
. the universe has fallen closer-closer . I know
because we share a heart . beat as the pavement
rushes further in greeting . I am not blues I am

not yellows . I am not solid . not a liquid . I am the answer .

I am the space beyond stars

♯
D
4
D
E
5
7

◇

voyage

well the dock's far off so bets are off

now i navigate my mind

where calm is often hard to find

but i must surely leave behind

the worries that have led me here

when the storm breaks the sky is clear

when i'm afraid the less i fear

but now that i am getting strong

less often does it feel as wrong

and even when the days are long

i will still continue on

and cities rise and cities fall

at times we climb at times we crawl

but whether it's eternal

we exist in everything

and all the stars up in the sky

never have to wonder why

if our lives are but a lie

it is beautiful

for all that marvels when we die

we never have to say

goodb

♯
0
0
3
5
3
8

◇

arc

all
of
time
coexists

.

♯
D
6
D
6
D
6
◇

discovery

i don't know whether
life gets better
but i do know
this won't last forever
so why not find out

while it lasts

♯
8
C
A
A
8
7

eternity

longing for eternity unites us
across time and space
it is said the singularity shattered
and now we're billowing away into fragments
but what if they're facets
we're part of a diamond
ring revolving completion
the future a catalyst for the past
a spirit realizing existence
in its reflection

www.ingramcontent.com/pod-product-compliance
Lightning Source LLC
Chambersburg PA
CBHW050435010526
44118CB00013B/1544